D0290631

DK READERS

Pre-level 1

Fishy Tales
Colorful Days
Garden Friends
Party Fun

In the Park
Farm Animals
Cuentos de Peces *en español*
Dias llenos de color *en español*

Level 1

A Day at Greenhill Farm
Truck Trouble
Tale of a Tadpole
Surprise Puppy!
Duckling Days
A Day at Seagull Beach
Whatever the Weather
Busy Buzzy Bee
Big Machines
Wild Baby Animals
A Bed for the Winter
Born to be a Butterfly
Dinosaur's Day
Feeding Time
Diving Dolphin
Rockets and Spaceships
My Cat's Secret
First Day at Gymnastics

A Trip to the Zoo
I Can Swim!
A Trip to the Library
A Trip to the Doctor
LEGO: Trouble at the Bridge
LEGO: Secret at Dolphin Bay
Star Wars: What is a Wookiee?
A Day in the Life of a Builder
A Day in the Life of a Dancer
A Day in the Life of a Firefighter
A Day in the Life of a Teacher
A Day in the Life of a Musician
A Day in the Life of a Doctor
A Day in the Life of a Police Officer
A Day in the Life of a TV Reporter
Gigantes de Hierro *en español*
Crías del mundo animal *en español*

Level 2

Dinosaur Dinners
Fire Fighter!
Bugs! Bugs! Bugs!
Slinky, Scaly Snakes!
Animal Hospital
The Little Ballerina
Munching, Crunching, Sniffing,
  and Snooping
The Secret Life of Trees
Winking, Blinking, Wiggling,
  and Waggling
Astronaut: Living in Space
Twisters!
Holiday! Celebration Days
  around the World
The Story of Pocahontas
Horse Show
Survivors: The Night the Titanic
  Sank

Eruption! The Story of Volcanoes
The Story of Columbus
Journey of a Humpback Whale
Amazing Buildings
Feathers, Flippers, and Feet
Outback Adventure: Australian
  Vacation
Sniffles, Sneezes, Hiccups, and
  Coughs
LEGO: Castle Under Attack
LEGO: Rocket Rescue
Star Wars: Journey Through Space
MLB: A Batboy's Day
MLB: Let's Go to the Ballpark!
¡Insectos! *en español*
¡Bomberos! *en español*
Ice Skating Stars

A Note to Parents

DK READERS is a compelling program for beginning readers, designed in conjunction with leading literacy experts, including Dr. Linda Gambrell, Director of the Eugene T. Moore School of Education at Clemson University. Dr. Gambrell has served on the Board of Directors of the International Reading Association and as President of the National Reading Conference.

Beautiful illustrations and superb full-color photographs combine with engaging, easy-to-read stories to offer a fresh approach to each subject in the series. Each DK READER is guaranteed to capture a child's interest while developing his or her reading skills, general knowledge, and love of reading.

The five levels of DK READERS are aimed at different reading abilities, enabling you to choose the books that are exactly right for your child:

Pre-level 1: Learning to read
Level 1: Beginning to read
Level 2: Beginning to read alone
Level 3: Reading alone
Level 4: Proficient readers

The "normal" age at which a child begins to read can be anywhere from three to eight years old, so these levels are only a general guideline.

No matter which level you select, you can be sure that you are helping your child learn to read, then read to learn!

LONDON, NEW YORK, MUNICH,
MELBOURNE, AND DELHI

Series Editor Deborah Lock
U.S. Editor Elizabeth Hester
Senior Art Editor Sonia Moore
Production Allison Lenane
DTP Designer Almudena Díaz
Jacket Designer Katy Wall
Photographer Andy Crawford
Consultant Dr. Aviva Schein

Reading Consultant
Linda Gambrell, Ph.D.

First American Edition, 2005
05 06 07 08 09 10 9 8 7 6 5 4 3 2 1
Published in the United States by DK Publishing, Inc.
375 Hudson Street, New York, New York 10014

Published in Great Britain by Dorling Kindersley Limited

Library of Congress Cataloging-in-Publication Data
Lock, Deborah.
   A trip to the doctor / written by Deborah Lock.-- 1st American ed.
     p. cm. -- (Dk readers. Level 1)
   ISBN 0-7566-1137-7 (pb) -- ISBN 0-7566-1136-9 (plc)
   1. Children--Medical examinations--Juvenile literature. 2. Children-
-Preparation for medical care--Juvenile literature. I. Title. II. Dorling
Kindersley readers. 1, Beginning to read
   RJ50.5.L63 2005
   618.92'0075--dc22
                            2005001089

Color reproduction by Colourscan, Singapore
Printed and bound in China by L Rex Printing Co., Ltd.

Photographs taken at Brentfield Medical Centre
with thanks to Dr. Roland Hughes.
Thanks also to all the models: Freddie Feltham, Su Yin Chan,
Gillian Flashman, and Michelle Gibbins.
Many thanks to "Bearwithlove.com" for their loan of the doctor
and get-well teddy bears. Thanks also to P.C.Werth Ltd.
for their loan of the audiology equipment, and to
the Scrub Factory™ for the nurse's uniform.

All other images © Dorling Kindersley Limited
For further information see: www.dkimages.com

Discover more at
www.dk.com

 **READERS**

BEGINNING
1
TO READ

A Trip to the Doctor

Written by Deborah Lock

DK Publishing, Inc.

Jake was brushing his teeth
after breakfast.
"Are you ready?" called Mom.
"Your checkup with
the doctor is today."

"But I feel fine!"
said Jake,
hurrying into the hall.

At the doctor's office,
Jake and Mom went to the
reception [re-SEP-shun] desk.
The receptionist checked Jake's
name on her records.

"Please take a seat
in the waiting room,"
said the receptionist.

receptionist

Jake sat down and read his book.
After a few minutes, a nurse
came and called Jake's name.

"I'll check a few things first
and then your doctor
will see you," said the nurse.

nurse

In the checkup room,
Jake took off his shoes.
He stepped onto the scale.

scale

Then he stood against
the height chart.
The nurse wrote down
the numbers on Jake's medical
[MED-i-cal] records.

The nurse said, "Now I'll check how well your heart is pumping blood through your body."

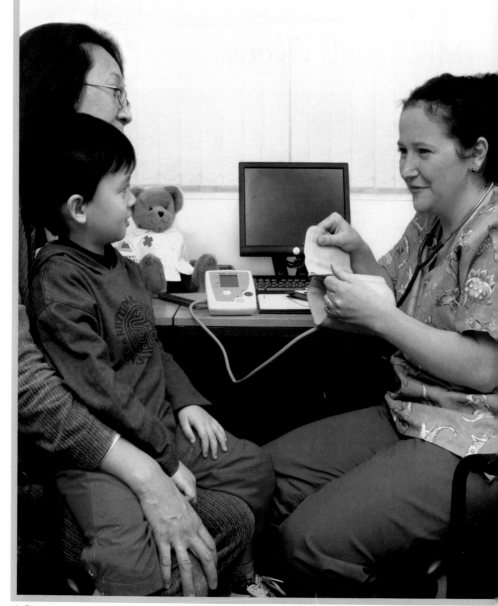

She put a cuff on Jake's arm.
"It's like a small balloon," she said.
It became tighter and tighter
as it filled with air.

The nurse watched the numbers
on the meter as the cuff began
to lose air.
"That's healthy!" said the nurse.

Then she took Jake's temperature
[TEM-pur-a-chure] using
a thermometer [ther-MOM-i-ter].

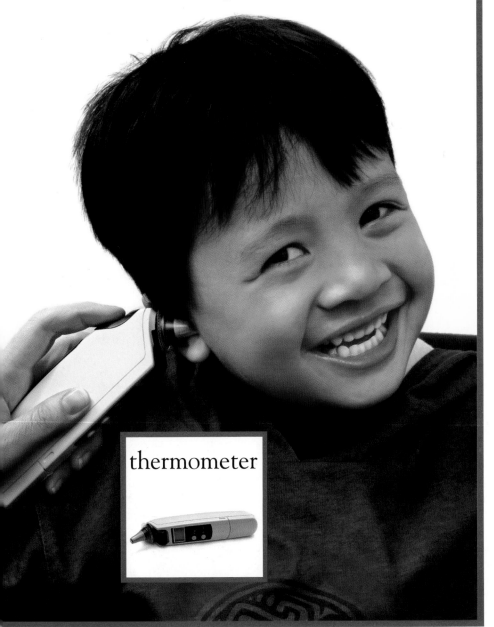

thermometer

"Hello, Jake," said Dr. Hill,
as she entered the room.
She looked at Jake's records.

"You look well.
Is your diet
healthy?"
she asked.

doctor

16

"I eat fruit and vegetables every day," said Jake.

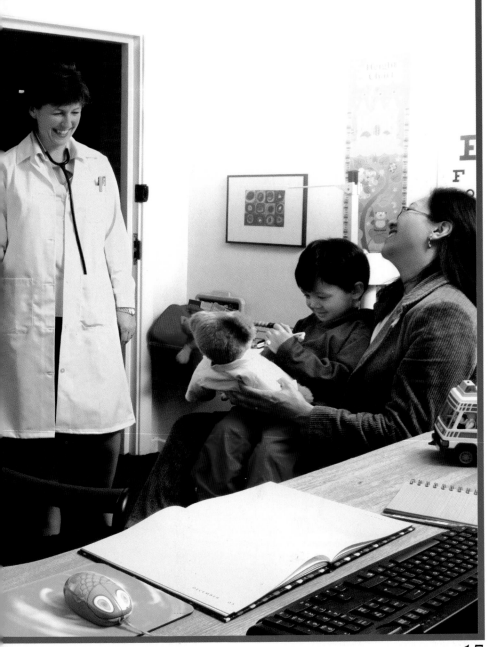

"I'll be checking to see that
your body is working just right,"
said Dr. Hill.
"This is a stethoscope
[STETH-a-scope].
It lets me hear your heartbeat
and your lungs."
She pressed the round,
cool part against
Jake's chest and back.

stethoscope

Dr. Hill checked Jake's ears,
nose, and mouth.
Jake sat very still.

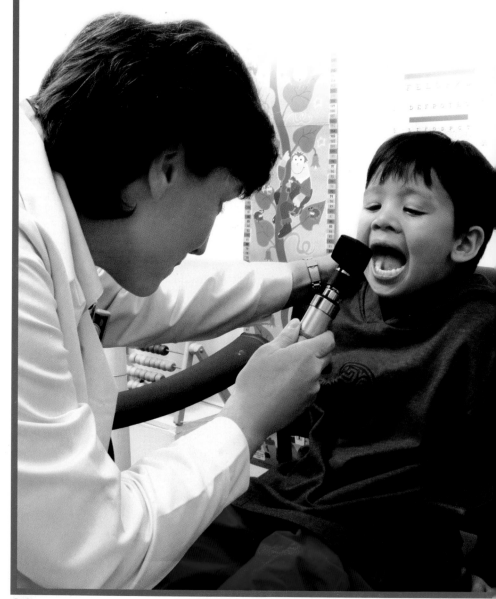

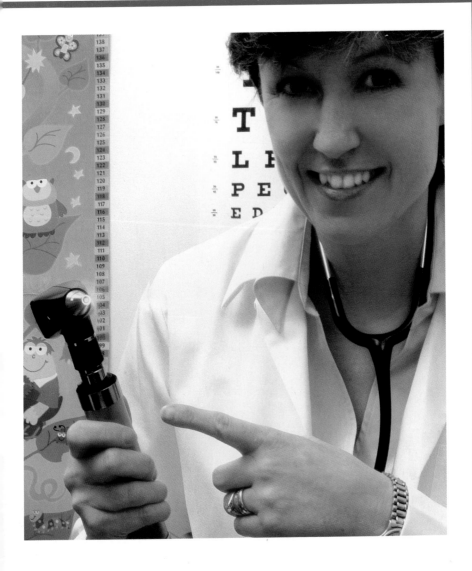

"This light helps me to see
if there are any infections
[in-FEK-shunz]," Dr. Hill said.
"I'm also checking your teeth."

Dr. Hill checked different
parts of Jake's body.
"These all look and feel
healthy," she said.
"Do you exercise every day?"

"I ride my bicycle," said Jake.
"Do you wear a helmet?"
asked Dr. Hill.
Jake nodded.

helmet

"Now I'll check how well you can hear and see," said Dr. Hill.
Jake put on some earphones.

He pointed to the ear
where he heard a sound.

earphones

25

Jake read some letters
on a wall chart.

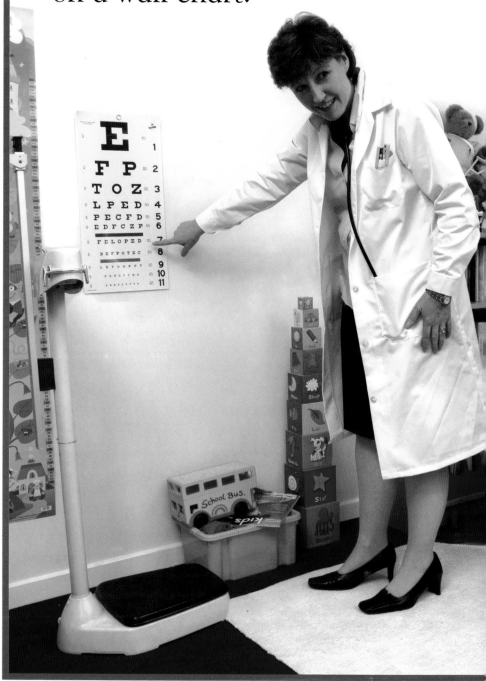

He covered one eye
and then the other.
"Remember, watching television
can strain your eyes," said
Dr. Hill, "so don't watch too
much or sit too close."

"Now, do you have any questions?" asked Dr. Hill. "Is Jake up-to-date with his booster shots?" asked Mom.

Dr. Hill nodded.

Jake talked to Dr. Hill about how he was doing at school.

Outside the doctor's office,
Jake said to his Mom,

"It was smart to meet Dr. Hill.
Now she'll know all about me
when I am sick."

"Good-bye!"

Picture word list

receptionist
page 7

doctor
page 16

nurse
page 9

stethoscope
page 18

scale
page 10

helmet
page 23

thermometer
page 15

earphones
page 25

 **READERS**

My name is

_____

I have read this book ☑

Date

_____